Making Your Way To GOD

Orlease King

MAKING YOUR WAY TO GOD. Copyright © 2020. Orlease King. All Rights Reserved.

No rights claimed for public domain material, all rights reserved. No parts of this publication may be reproduced, stored in any retrieval system, or transmitted in any form or by any means, electronic, mechanical, recording, or otherwise, without the prior written permission of the author. Violations may be subject to civil or criminal penalties.

ISBN: 978-1-949343-94-6 (paperback)

Printed in the United States of America

Scriptures taken from the Holy Bible, New International Version®, NIV®. Copyright © 1973, 1978, 1984, 2011 by Biblica, Inc.™ Used by permission of Zondervan. All rights reserved worldwide. www.zondervan.com. The "NIV" and "New International Version" are trademarks registered in the United States Patent and Trademark Office by Biblica, Inc.™

Hopefully you have this book in your hand because you love the Lord and you desire to know Him better and commit your life to Him.

OR

Maybe you are not even sure why you chose to read it, but something inside of you is curious or has a void that needs to be filled.

Whether you know it or not...

You are one step closer in your pursuit of God.

About This Book

This book was an assignment from God that I received through a vision on Monday April 13, 2020 amid a world pandemic known as Corona Virus (Covid_19).

God spoke to me whilst I was asleep that morning. He placed a book in my hand and instructed me to deliver the message contained therein. He vividly revealed the cover and title of the book and spoke **Isaiah 55:6** to me.

When I woke up, He further instructed me to read the entire Chapter of Isaiah 55. He unlocked the meaning of each verse to me in a special way and revealed how each verse was to be used to make up the contents.

This book is a guide for persons who are like I was before I accepted Jesus Christ as my Savior.

It is for those who love God and have always loved Him but are uncertain about making a commitment to Him.

It will help to take you on a one-step-at-a-time walk toward your calling, and help you discover the best friendship you will ever have, as well as lead you into the best life you could ever dream of.

Seek the Lord while he may be found; call on him while he is near.

Isaiah 55:6

This is one of the most popular verses in the Bible, spoken by the Prophet Isaiah in the Old Testament.

It is also at the core of my inspiration for this book.

If a person wants to obtain a true relationship with God, it must be sought. No one becomes His friend without desiring the friendship.

It is important to understand the nature of God. Every living human being has access to

Him through His Son Jesus Christ and the gift of the Holy Spirit. However, He will never force His way into our lives. Instead, He gives us the freedom to decide whether we want Him in it or not.

If ever you feel a distance between yourself and God, it does not mean God is not present. Rather it is you who have either stepped away from Him or completely shut Him out. He loves you too much to ever leave or forsake you. He is always close by, just waiting for you to invite Him into your heart.

The encouragement from Isaiah: *"Seek the Lord while he may be found"* implies that there will come a time when it will be impossible to access God or any of His great benefits. I really do not want to be the bearer of bad news, but it is a fact that you will not always be able to find him.

We have but only a lifetime to seek, find and accept God into our hearts. This could be good news, if only you knew how long it will be before you die.

I pray that you understand that you must die and, like everyone else on this earth, you do not know when exactly that day will be. If anyone should die without receiving forgiveness for their sins or without accepting the provision of mercy and salvation through Christ, then it will be too late to find God.

Just as people are destined to die once, and after that to face the judgement.

Hebrews 9:27

Simply put, this Bible verse makes it clear that after death there will be no other opportunity to correct any wrong done whilst you were alive. You will be judged solely upon the life you lived. Are you comfortable with that thought?

Once more Jesus said to them, "I am going, and you will look for me, and you will die in your sin. Where I go you cannot come."

John 8:21

Jesus spoke these words to explain that all those who reject Him must die without their sins forgiven. Where He is, they cannot go, for no sin can enter heaven. There is no way of pardon but by Him.

Isaiah further urges us to: *"call on him while he is near."* This is not to say God is only near to us on specific occasions but rather mankind sometimes has a more favorable opportunity to experience His presence through certain occurrences or occasions. For example, when we hear the Gospel being preached and it presses on our conscience; when you are sick, and God delivers you through healing; when your marriage is headed for ruin and God saves it; when we lose a family member or a dear friend to death and you mourn and seek comfort. Indeed, any of these instances will shift our focus towards God and surely if we seek Him then we will find Him. I am by no means suggesting that God can only be found in moments of sickness or tragedy. Many have also found Him in moments of celebration and happiness. Whenever you feel Him nearest, take hold of Him in that moment, since you know not your last hour.

The Bible warns in Hebrews 3 :15, **"As has just been said: "Today, if you hear his voice, do not harden your hearts as you did in the rebellion.""**

Contents

About This Book v
ACKNOWLEDGMENTS..13
DEDICATION 15
CHAPTER ONE:
How Do I Know That God Is With Me?...............19
CHAPTER TWO:
Brand New Future, Brand New Hope..................29
CHAPTER THREE:
Alignment And Influences......................................41
    Why Do I Need Church?................................48
CHAPTER FOUR:
Chosen For A Cause, Filled With Purpose 59
CHAPTER FIVE:
Victory 71
    What Do I Need To Do To Be Saved? 74
    No One Knows My Struggles 76
WHAT THE BIBLE SAYS...83
ABOUT YOU 83

The Enemy No Longer Has Power Over You 85

Invitation to the Thirsty 91

ABOUT THE AUTHOR 95

    AUTHORS NOTES 97

ACKNOWLEDGMENTS

To my Lord and Savior, Jesus Christ, who rescued me from sin and destruction, I thank Him for the gift of the Holy Spirit, who has been my guide in the production of this book and in all areas of my everyday life.

From the beginning I have had the support and encouragement of some beautiful persons who believe there is greatness in all human beings and strive to grow and help others grow. Thanks to these persons, we have a clear demonstration that there is great hope for the future of this world. One such person worthy of mentioning is Sally-Ann Gray, International Award-Winning Author and Educator, who is also a genuine friend and motivator. She has freely given me her time, knowledge, and expertise. For this I extend heartfelt gratitude and immense love and appreciation.

To my editing and publishing team, thanks for making the vision a reality.

To my parents, Norma and Junior, who never stopped believing in me; thank you is simply not enough. I love you so much.

To my Aunt Marlene, who vividly depicts what it means to be a great soul. Thank you.

To my Pastors and church family, thanks for holding my hands as I make my way to God. To everyone who has ever said to me, "You can do all things through Christ who strengthens you." You have all provided me with a fantastic opportunity to lead a great group of people into the best life they can have.

THANK YOU

DEDICATION

This book is dedicated to my niece, Toni-Ann Samuels, whom I believe to be my spiritual assignment.

She is a courageous teenager in passionate pursuit of Christ.

My dear child, like I have always told you, Jesus Christ sees and knows the heart. He sees your commitment to Him and is pleased.

Baby girl, always remember that God is with you every step of the way. If you ever feel like you are alone, just like the light switch brings light into a dark room, so does the Word of God.

So, when it gets dark in the room of your life, in the same way you know where to find the switch in your bedroom and flick it on to get light when your bedroom is dark, so too you should know how to find God's Word, His promises, His truths and speak them from your heart to bring His light, His comfort, His joy and His peace to your life.

STAY FEARLESS "Tweedy Bird," you have a generation to lead.

Love Always,

Aunty

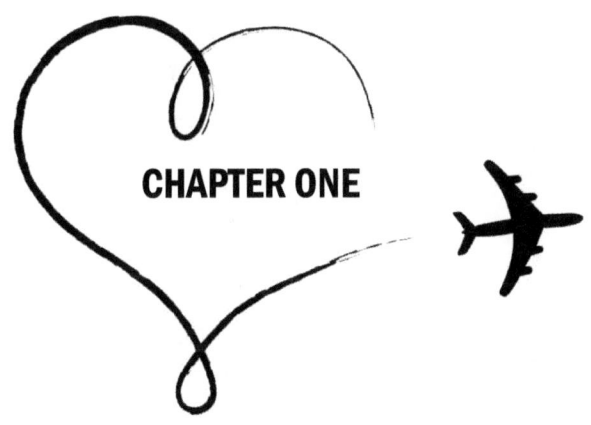

CHAPTER ONE

"We need to find God, and he cannot be found in noise and restlessness. God is the friend of silence. See how nature - trees, flowers, grass - grows in silence; see the stars, the moon and the sun, how they move in silence... We need silence to be able to touch souls."

Mother Teresa

How Do I Know That God Is With Me?

Have you ever been in a situation where you were about to go somewhere or do something, then suddenly changed your mind about going or doing it, only to find out later that your decision spared you from trouble? Often your response to such an experience would be, "Thank you Jesus."

Such a response is correct. God sent us His Son, Jesus Christ, to be our Savior. The Holy Spirit is given to us, through Jesus Christ, to be our guide and shield.

Even while in sin, the Spirit of God is with us constantly guiding us, although, because we are captivated by sin, we ignore the presence and the voice of God.

You know when I sit and when I rise; you perceive my thoughts from afar. You discern my going out and my lying down; you are familiar with all my ways. Before a word is on my tongue you, Lord, know it completely.

– Psalm 139:2-4

This is how well God knows you, and He knows all of this about you because He is always present with you. Do not forget that He made you. Nothing that you do will ever surprise Him. Therefore, He is not angry with you when you sin. Instead, He waits for you to confess your sins to Him so He can swiftly forgive you.

When you constantly sin and choose to live that way without giving any regard to God; never confessing, never asking for mercy and forgiveness, never changing your mind from the way of sin to the way of God, that is when you really hurt Him. It was never God's intention for mankind to be separated from

Him. God loves you and wants you to be His very own child.

Activity 1:

Read Psalms 139 today and be reassured and encouraged that **GOD IS WITH YOU!**

Use the space provided to document the verse or verses that speaks to you most.

_____
_____
_____
_____
_____
_____
_____
_____
_____
_____
_____
_____
_____

_____
_____
_____
_____
_____
_____
_____
_____
_____
_____
_____
_____

Reflect on specific times when you knew for sure that **God was with you**.

Note a few of these experiences below

_____
_____
_____
_____
_____
_____
_____

Orlease King

Making Your Way To God

Write a simple "Thank You" message to God. Be very specific about what you are thanking Him for.

Make note of the date and time when your message is written.

_____
_____
_____
_____
_____
_____
_____
_____
_____
_____
_____
_____
_____
_____
_____
_____
_____

Orlease King

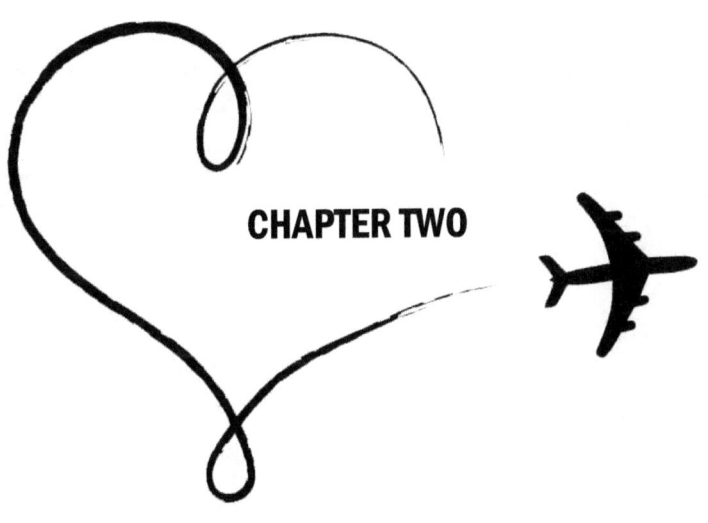

CHAPTER TWO

"What God intended for you goes far beyond anything you can imagine."

Oprah Winfrey

Brand New Future, Brand New Hope

Imagine owing someone a huge sum of money, which you are unable to pay. The person asks you for payment and you decide to be honest and sincere. So, you tell the truth that you really can't pay because you have no money. Now, imagine that this person who has every right to be angry with you, instead says, "It's okay, I understand. There is no need to pay me back. I will totally forget that you owe me and if you need anything, I'm here to help."

Now, let us be realistic. When you decide to confess your sins to God and turn your life over to Him, God will do exactly what that person you owed did.

HE WILL ERASE ALL YOUR PAST SINS AND GIVE YOU A BRAND-NEW START.

He does not treat us as our sins deserve or repay us according to our iniquities. For as high as the heavens are above the earth, so great is his love for those who fear him; as far as the east is from the west, so far has he removed our transgressions from us.

Psalms 103:10-12

You are offered a fresh start that is yours to keep and enjoy. You can now rewrite your story. God is now completely in charge of your life. That is how He responds to those who choose Him. Even if you are uncertain about what that new way of life should look like or where exactly to start, He promises to make it clear to you.

This is what the Lord says— your Redeemer, the Holy One of Israel: "I am the LORD your God, who teaches you what is best for you, who directs you in the way you should go."

Isaiah 48:17

Many times, a person who loves God and wants to give his/her life to Him might hesitate because he/she is not sure what to do after he/she surrenders to Him. They have a fear that they might fail in their efforts to please God. You probably feel exactly that way too.

Guess what? You really do not need to worry. This is where **trust** comes in. You must trust God and His promises. He is your Tour Guide on this journey, so your main duty is to trust Him.

You will sin, at some point, we all do. But He refreshes you each new day so long as you abide with Him and be honest about your weaknesses.

Choosing to give your life to God guarantees you full access to Him and full benefit of all His promises. Therefore, you need not worry about your future.

Trust in the Lord with all your heart, and lean not on your own understanding; in all your ways submit to him, and he will make your paths straight.

Proverbs 3:5-6

Our pasts are all different and some are way too ugly and horrible to forget. The harder you focus on forgetting past pain, sorrow, rejection, abuse, and hardships, the more they will sit at the front of your mind. The more you focus on the newness you have received through Christ and take this opportunity to rewrite your script, the further away you will push those haunting memories. Because God already knows this will not be easy to do, He has made Himself available to take you through the process.

Often, we hear some of the biggest success stories about people who had some of the most traumatic beginnings. Their life may have started out in unfavorable conditions. Yet, somehow, life took them on a completely different journey to achieve greatness. God can use even your past hurt to shape a prosperous future. It is just a part of who He is and how He takes care of those who belong to Him.

I will instruct you and teach you in the way you should go; I will counsel you with my loving eye on you.

Psalm 32:8

Not only will God direct you, but also stay right there with you and watch with loving eyes as you take each step.

In Jeremiah 29:11 God tells us, in no uncertain terms, that everyone who believes in Him, accepts, and obeys Him shall prosper. He had you in mind when He made this promise so do not let your past or present cause you to doubt your future.

This promise is YOURS and it is sealed with a kiss from God.

"**For I know the plans I have for you,**" declares the L**ORD**, "**plans to prosper you and not to harm you, plans to give you hope and a future.**"

Jeremiah 29:11

Activity 11

Write in the space provided below some promises you want to make to yourself for the future.

Make note of the date and time when your message is written.

_____
_____
_____
_____
_____
_____
_____
_____
_____
_____

Orlease King

Making Your Way To God

Write some promises you want to make to God.

Make note of the date and time when your message is written

_____
_____
_____
_____
_____
_____
_____
_____
_____
_____
_____
_____
_____
_____
_____
_____
_____
_____

Orlease King

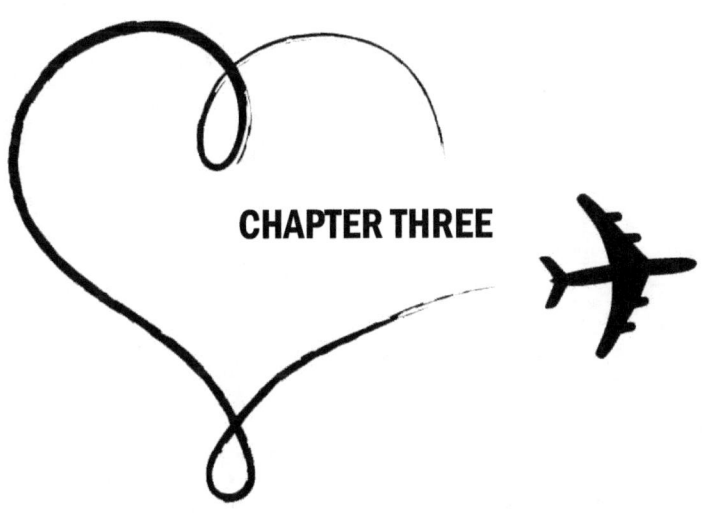

CHAPTER THREE

"I don't stand for the black man's side, I don't stand for the white man's side. I stand for God's side."

Bob Marley

Alignment And Influences

Often, we think we have our lives in order based on plans we have made for our education, career, or family. We think we know exactly what is best for us. Maybe at this point in your life God has indeed put some thoughts in your mind about what He wants you to do with your life. However, because those thoughts belong to Him originally, He must be allowed to organize and execute them His way. If you choose to do it without God, your chances of error are inevitable. Factors such as confusion or distractions will step in, slow you down, throw you off and ruin your plan, if you do not have the right influences to hold you accountable and keep you on course. The things that you want do not matter as much as what God wants for you. To obtain a life of success, you must be properly aligned.

"For my thoughts are not your thoughts, neither are your ways my ways," declares the Lord. "As the heavens are higher than the earth, so are my ways higher than your ways and my thoughts than your thoughts."

Isaiah 55:8-9

No human can think or act the way God does. His thoughts and ways are simply far better than ours. Trying to figure out life without God and depending on your own brilliance is not likely to produce the best results. God will shuffle some things around in your life to help you be your best self and to keep you steady on the journey with Him. No Christian can survive the journey all by him/herself.

Remember, even after accepting Jesus in your life and being saved by Him, you will still be living in a world where you are surrounded by sin and old influences that will taunt, tempt and tease you. Trying to fight these attacks with pure physical willpower and resistance is not enough to keep them off. What you will need is a good circle of people to help you fight spiritually. You will need the right people in your life to pray with you, enforce the Word of God, support and encourage you along the way; persons who will not be judgmental but will share their personal stories of failures so you have good examples of how to identify your errors and get pass them; persons who love God and demonstrate their love and loyalty towards Him in their everyday lifestyle. They will not be easy to find, but trust God to take you through the process and make the right connections at the right times. Often, we feel as though the people we have been friends with the longest are best for us. Sadly, your best friend from high school might not be a part of your new alignment. You must be willing to "let go and let God" work; just embrace the changes in your life.

No ambitious human being desires to exit this world in the same state that he/she entered it. Picture yourself being born as a baby, living to age eighty, still looking like a baby, wearing baby clothes and still suckling your mother. Ridiculous, right?

Usain St. Leo Bolt, the world's fastest man and greatest sprinter of all time, once stated: *"People look at you strange saying you changed. Like you worked that hard to stay the same."*

His statement is very profound. Expect people to be surprised about your changes. Any great achievement comes with sacrifices and changes. Choosing a life with Christ is an extremely great achievement. Therefore, people will question the changes that come with your success.

You must be aligned with the right people, and you will also need to disconnect from certain environments and materials. This might not be easy, but you must remember the

Orlease King

promise that God gave you: He is with you the entire way.

Why do you have to give up so much? Because you are about to gain so much more.

The importance of these adjustments is to help in guarding your mind, which is your most valuable and vulnerable asset. Your mind is what Satan, who is your enemy, is after. So it must be guarded at all costs. Remember that when you make the choice to give your life to God, an entire renewal process will take place at that very moment. Your mind will be transformed, it will be set on all the right things and Satan will do everything in his power to get you back to where you were. In order to keep your mind right, you will have to feed your mind right. If you are still going to places that promote ungodly behavior, reading materials with ungodly influences, watching the types of movies that provoke ungodly thoughts and emotions, engaging in games or conversations that are not wrapped up in Biblical truth, these are all recipes for disaster when you are not spiritually mature.

The good news is, whatever God removes, He will replace with something even better. Which means your suspicion that this new life will be boring is wrong. He will find you appropriate social and entertainment gatherings, He will reveal to you television programs, movies and all other engaging activities that are right for you, you will have a whole new circle of friends to get to know, who will also introduce you to new things and places with Godly influences. It is an exciting adventure and you will discover so much, especially about yourself: things like your talents and giftings that you were never able to activate before. Do not be surprised if you run into great personal or professional opportunities. Just be patient along the way and always consult with God about areas of uncertainty (never forget that you have a personal tour guide – the Holy Spirit). When you trust and obey God and allow Him to properly align you with the right people, you will start making headway on your journey.

Walk with the wise and become wise, for a companion of fools suffers harm.

Proverbs 13:20

Wrong influences results in bad decisions, so you should thank God for rearranging your alignments. Well known international pastor, Andy Stanley, in his Study Guide titled, *"Guardrails"* revealed this frightening fact based on an article written by Neuroscientist Moran Cerf: "The more we study engagement, we see time and time again that just being next to certain people actually aligns your brain with them." This information certainly urges us to be more mindful of whom we hang with.

A very crucial piece of alignment that you will need to have is a good Bible-based church to become your church home with a loving church family. Do not wander around trying to find one. You should start your search by first praying to God specifically about aligning you with the church that is appropriate for you. I prayed hard about this at the start of my journey and surely God has blessed me with the most wonderful church home and family. However, if you don't find one immediately, please don't let that be your reason for giving up. In the meantime, become a part of a small Christian group, which conducts Bible studies and other activities that revolve around the Bible. There are several of them around and they are a good way to get you started since the group is smaller and gives way for one-on-one teaching and understanding. However, note that being a member of a church is particularly important and should not be substituted.

Why Do I Need Church?

How often have you heard the statement, "The same God who is at church is also in my house?" It is frequently used as an excuse for not going to church. Maybe you have even said it before. I did, before I received Christ. So yes, the same God who is in the church is in your house, but are the same influences and distractions that are in your house in the church? Most likely not. Remember now that Satan wants full control of your mind. So, if he can keep you out of the house of God, then he has a better opportunity to do that. No one will willingly give themselves to the enemy, especially not you because in your heart you know you love God. So, it is best to be in the company of others who genuinely love Him too. Furthermore, it is written in the Bible, which is our manual for maintaining a proper relationship with God.

And let us consider how we may spur one another on toward love and good deeds, not giving up meeting together, as some are in the habit of doing, but encouraging one another — and all the more as you see the Day approaching.

Hebrews 10:24-24

We need each other. Meeting together gives us the opportunity to strengthen and encourage each other. It pleases God for us to do this. In fact, He warns us not to forsake this gathering together with one another.

That is, that you and I may be mutually encouraged by each other's faith.

Romans 1:12

For just as each of us has one body with many members, and these members do not all have the same function, so in Christ we, though many, form one body, and each member belongs to all the others.

Romans 12:4-5

Just as your physical body requires your arms, legs and all the other members to function best, so too does the church represent the body of Christ. Every member has a function that is crucial to its existence.

Activity III

Make a list below of all the persons in your current circle.

Next to each name write one admirable trait of the person that aligns well with your future goals.

_____
_____
_____
_____
_____
_____
_____
_____
_____
_____
_____
_____
_____
_____

Making Your Way To God

Now try to identify three persons on your list, based on their traits, that can best help you get to where you are going.

Spend some time reflecting. Is your circle too big, too small, or not in keeping with helping you to achieve the best that life has to offer you?

Make notes as you see fit.

_____
_____
_____
_____
_____
_____
_____
_____
_____
_____
_____
_____
_____

Making Your Way To God

Orlease King

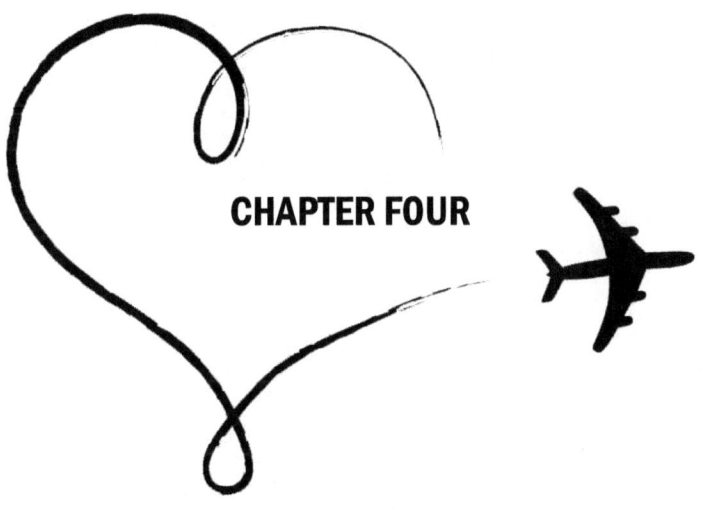

CHAPTER FOUR

"While I know myself as a creation of God, I am also obligated to realize and remember that everyone else and everything else are also God's creation."

Maya Angelou

Chosen For A Cause, Filled With Purpose

Wherever you are right now, I challenge you to look around you. Look at different items that are in sight. If you are at home, look at that rug on the floor, the curtains at the window, maybe you can see a bed or television or the toilet. If you are outdoors, you are probably seeing a type of fruit tree, a building or a car. Wherever you are and whatever you are looking at, that thing was created and exists for a specific purpose. Whomever it belongs to selected it to use it for the purpose which it was made.

I know you will not use a television to cover the window or a toilet to sleep on because you know that is not what they were made to do. But how do you know this? Because the person who invented these items gave specific instructions on what they are for and how they should function. There is a manual or some type of guide about the function or operation of each item.

You are no different; God, who knows the purpose for which you were made, created you. There is a written manual called, ***"The Holy Bible"*** that outlines all the details about how you were created and the instructions for your operation on earth. This is why God is calling you to Him and why He waits diligently for you to answer His call, so that He can freely reveal to you how you can get the best out of life. Stop running around in circles on your own trying to find satisfaction which is costing you much frustration, grief, and confusion.

Come, all you who are thirsty, come to the waters; and you who have no money, come, buy and eat! Come, buy wine and milk without money and without cost. Why spend money on what is not bread, and your labor

on what does not satisfy? Listen, listen to me, and eat what is good, and you will delight in the richest of fare.

Isaiah 55:1-2

There is a reason why you are here, and God knew it even before you got here. This is why He chose you to be a part of His Kingdom. He has not kept anything about you a secret. All of it is written in the Bible but you must hunger and thirst enough for Him and His truth to then start feeding on it. Only then will you see what He already knows about you. You were made for a specific purpose and the sooner you realize this, the more rewarding your life will be. It would be sad to spend all your life living in this world, then die not knowing why you were here in the first place.

Discovering your purpose in life is one of the fundamental factors of fulfillment and happiness. Without it, you will live life less focused, less efficient and you will always feel a need to be searching for something, because you do not feel connected to the things you do.

God wants to use you to change the world. You were born for such a purpose; you live and breathe for such a cause. So, if you ever thought that your obscure, little life can leave no mark on this world, you have no idea just how wrong you are. Your existence has already impacted our world. Daily you leave indelible impressions on the people around you. Your interactions with others affect the timing of events or their ideas and decisions either in a good or bad way. Lives are changed for better or worse by how you live the life you are given. As creatures made in God's own image and likeness, all human beings are given real power to change the course of history through what we say and do. If you knew the power you possess, you would never question the big plans God has for your life, nor your ability to greatly impact nations. He wants to trust you with the power you have, knowing you will not use it for evil but for His purpose.

Surely you will summon nations you know not, and nations you do not know will come running to you, because of the LORD your God, the Holy One of Israel, for he has endowed you with splendor.

Isaiah 55:5

There is so much in you and many persons are dependent on it all. The only problem is that you cannot do it all without God. You must seek Him first.

Give ear and come to me; listen, that you may live. I will make an everlasting covenant with you, my faithful love promised to David.

Isaiah 55:3

God is saying, just come to Him, obey Him and He will make you a promise that lasts forever, just as He did for David. David was only a young boy when Samuel anointed him, promising that God would one day make him a great king. David tended sheep for years, waiting on God. Then things happened.

At about 14 to 16 years of age, David volunteered to fight a giant named Goliath using only a sling. David trusted in God and with his faith and a sling he killed Goliath. Saul, who was the reigning king at that time, made David an army commander and David excelled in Saul's army. David later became the King of Israel (See 1 Samuel 17-18 and 2 Samuel 5).

Whatever God has set out for you to do, He will equip you with all that is needed to get the job done. Many laughed at David who was facing the giant with only a sling and a few stones. But David knew that God was with him, so he was not just depending on his own abilities. He trusted the power of God that was in him. God is faithful to deliver whatever He promises.

As the rain and the snow come down from heaven, and do not return to it without watering the earth and making it bud and flourish, so that it yields seed for the sower and bread for the eater, so is my word that goes out from my mouth: It will not return to me empty, but will accomplish what I desire and achieve the purpose for which I sent it.

Isaiah 55:10-11

How wonderful it is to know that you belong to a God who will never disappoint you; a God who designed you with power and purpose.

Activity IV

Do you think that you have positively impacted the lives of those around you?

Highlight the most appropriate answer:

Absolutely YES

I am not sure

Sometimes

I have never thought about my impact on them

Is there a burning passion that you have inside that could make a difference in someone's life or to this world?

Write a prayer to God about it.

_____
_____
_____
_____
_____
_____
_____
_____
_____
_____
_____
_____
_____

Orlease King

Making Your Way To God

CHAPTER FIVE

"I believe God is managing affairs and that He doesn't need any advice from me. With God in charge, I believe everything will work out for the best in the end. So what is there to worry about."

Henry Ford

Victory

When athletes enter a race, all will run, but not all will receive a prize at the end of the race. Only winners are rewarded and obtain honor. Therefore, each participant must train and prepare well before race day. Each must run with passion, desire, and determination to win. In the same way, though everyone has life, some will live it more rewardingly. Those who live life purposefully, have a high level of discipline, specific goals they are aiming for and a deeper reason for why they do what they do.

When you persistently and passionately pursue God's presence, you are destined to discover His purpose for your life and will ultimately achieve victory in what you do. True victory is not limited to the acquisition of earthly riches. If you have a Father in heaven who loves you unconditionally, a relationship with Jesus that cannot be broken, the Word of God abiding in your heart and an eternal home in heaven with your name on it, then you are living a victorious life.

Do you not know that in a race all the runners run, but only one gets the prize? Run in such a way as to get the prize. Everyone who competes in the game goes into strict training. They do it to get a crown that will not last, but we do it to get a crown that will last forever. Therefore I do not run like someone running aimlessly; I do not fight like a boxer beating the air.

1 Corinthians 9:24-26

Dr. Charles Stanley, International Pastor and founder of In Touch Ministries, also the father of Pastor Andy Stanley, posed this question in one of his sermons: "When you, in the last five minutes of your life are dying, how much good will your automobiles and your houses and your bank account, your stocks and bonds, even your friends; how much is anything in all this life going to matter when you've got five minutes and you have everything, but God?"

He then advised: "My friend, don't wait till it's too late and you realize that life is over and what you've sunk your whole life into is meaningless, purposeless, transient, passing and you are about to leave it all behind."

Dr. Stanley's question is a very worrying thought for one who has not yet given his/her life to God and has not dedicated him/herself to doing His work. If you have given all of yourself to the things of this world only for earthly returns, then it would be like throwing your coins to the bottom of a well, with no hope of ever retrieving them.

Don't you not know that when you offer yourselves to someone as obedient slaves, you are slaves of the one you obey - whether

you are slaves to sin, which leads to death, or to obedience, which leads to righteousness?

Romans 6:16

You become what you yield to and now that you know this, you have the opportunity to redirect your choices. Hopefully, since you have read your way through this book and have gotten all the way to this chapter, you are making some positive steps towards victory.

What Do I Need To Do To Be Saved?

A prison warder once asked this same question in Acts 16:30.

Paul and Silas had been beaten and thrown into prison with their feet fastened in a restraining device. They were unable to sleep because of the discomfort they were experiencing so they sang praises to God throughout the night. At midnight, as they were praying, there was an earthquake that broke them loose from their bonds and opened the prison doors. The Prison Warder rushed over and saw the doors opened. He assumed that the prisoners had fled. The law in those times stated that a warder who lost prisoners should be put to death, so he was about to commit suicide. Paul called out to him and stopped him from doing himself any harm because they were all still there. Upon hearing this news, the Warder fell before Paul, trembling and pleading, *"Sirs, what must I do to be saved?"* Paul and Silas both responded: *"Believe in the Lord Jesus, and you will be saved — you and your household."* As a result of this conversation, not only did the Warder believe but his entire house also believed and was saved (See Acts 16:30-31).

The simple answer given to that Prison Warder is the answer to your question also. For it is only through faith (which is believing) that you will receive grace (which is kindness) from Jesus Christ. He will then pour out His favor upon you and free you from all your sins. You cannot buy this freedom; you cannot work for it. There is nothing of your own might and power that you can do to be saved. It is a gift that only God can give.

For it is by grace you have been saved, through faith—and this is not from yourselves, it is the gift of God— not by works, so that no one can boast. For we are God's handiwork, created in Christ Jesus to do good works, which God prepared in advance for us to do.

Ephesians 2:8-10

No One Knows My Struggles

You may say your situation is different. You may doubt your ability to function and maintain a normal life if you make a switch. You may think your mess is much too deep to get over suddenly. Your thought may be, "People don't know how hard it is to break my habits." That is not the issue at all. The questions you need to be asking yourself are:

"Does God know all of my struggles? Can God help me? Can God give me the victory?

Does God know how hard it is for me to depart from sin?" Of course God knows. He has delivered thousands who were in a worse state than you are.

Nothing is impossible for God. If He has been there for you up to this point in your life, what makes you think He would not carry you through now, especially now that you are making Him your choice?

The Apostle Paul explains in Romans 5 why, because of what Jesus Christ did on the cross, we who are now saved can live in peace and have hope for victory.

But God demonstrates his own love for us in this: While we were still sinners, Christ died for us. Since we have now been justified by his blood, how much more shall we be saved from God's wrath through him! For if, while we were God's enemies, we were reconciled

to him through the death of his Son, how much more, having been reconciled, shall we be saved through his life!

Romans 5:8-10

God knew your situation even before you knew it. He has already made a way to help you out of it. Even while you were not thinking about Him, He was thinking about you. He sent His Son to die for you, even before you loved Him. God wants you to have victory over everything holding you back. Just be honest with Him about your troubles, your fears and your struggles and He will take care of them.

1 John 1:9 says, **"If we confess our sins, he is faithful and just and will forgive us our sins and purify us from all unrighteousness."**

This is a perfect time to have that conversation with the one who loves you more than anyone else in this world could ever love you.

Giving your heart to God is as simple as having a sincere conversation with someone you love.

Right now, from the depth of your heart, say this prayer to God:

Almighty God, I surrender. In the name of Your Son, Jesus Christ, forgive me of all my sins. I choose Jesus Christ as my personal Savior. I believe He died for me and rose from the grave in victory and He lives within me. Take my life— all of it—and use me in Your holy service, in Jesus' name.
Amen.

Activity V

Now, privately, alone with God, kneel down and tell God all your problems, confess your sins to Him, talk aloud to Him as a little child, and believe He has forgiven you.

Document this moment with the date. It's the day you gave your life to God.

_____
_____
_____
_____
_____
_____

If you know that you have genuinely and sincerely done this, then know that God has also done His part.

YOU ARE FORGIVEN; YOU ARE SAVED!

Now go forth in **VICTORY**

You will go out in joy and be led forth in peace; the mountains and hills will burst into song before you, and all the trees of the field will clap their hands.

Isaiah 55:12

Orlease King

There is no promise that the journey ahead will be easy. But I can promise you that every sacrifice will be worth the reward of having Jesus Christ as your personal and constant friend.

For your body to be nourished and grow strong, healthy, and active, you must feed it well. Likewise, for your spirit to grow, be strengthened and keep active, you must feed it right.

Abide in the Word of God; get familiar with your Bible. Turn your attention to the things of God and sinful thoughts and behaviors will gradually depart from you.

In moments of uncertainty, take a journey through this book once again and reflect on all you have written in the note sections. But most importantly, journey through your mind and remember why you started this walk.

You are more than a conqueror, through Christ Jesus who strengthens you.

WHAT THE BIBLE SAYS ABOUT YOU

The Enemy No Longer Has Power Over You

The Bible consists of numerous spoken words from God through His prophets, apostles and Jesus Christ, who is the Son of God sent to represent God here on earth and to be a living example of the goodness of God. It will provide you with a daily reminder of who you are and whose you are.

Here are some truths the Bible reveals about you. Arm yourself with them so that when you are tested, you can throw them right back at your enemy, Satan, and defeat him.

The more we embrace these truths from the Scriptures about who we have become in Christ, the more stable, grateful, and fully assured we will be in this world.

I am a new creature in Christ.

Therefore, if anyone is in Christ, the new creation has come: The old has gone, the new is here! (2 Corinthians 5:17).

I am a child of God.

Yet to all who did receive him, to those who believed in his name, he gave the right to become children of God. (John 1:12).

I am a friend of Jesus.

I no longer call you servants, because a servant does not know his master's business. Instead, I have called you friends, for everything that I learned from my Father I have made known to you. (John 15:15).

I have been justified and redeemed.

And all are justified freely by his grace through the redemption that came by Christ Jesus. (Romans 3:24).

I will not be condemned by God.

Therefore, there is now no condemnation for those who are in Christ Jesus. (Romans 8:1).

I have been set free from the law of sin and death.

Because through Christ Jesus the law of the Spirit who gives life has set you free from the law of sin and death. (Romans 8:2).

I am joined to the Lord and am one spirit with Him.

But whoever is united with the Lord is one with him in spirit. (1 Corinthians 6:17).

I am chosen, holy, and blameless before God.

For he chose us in him before the creation of the world to be holy and blameless in his sight. In love. (Ephesians 1:4).

God loves me and has chosen me.

For we know, brothers and sisters loved by God, that he has chosen you. (1 Thessalonians 1:4).

I am God's workmanship, created to produce good works.

For we are God's handiwork, created in Christ Jesus to do good works, which God prepared in advance for us to do. (Ephesians 2:10).

My body is a temple of the Holy Spirit who dwells in me.

Do you not know that your bodies are temples of the Holy Spirit, who is in you, whom you have received from God? You are not your own. (1 Corinthians 6:19).

The peace of God guards my heart and mind.

And the peace of God, which transcends all understanding, will guard your hearts and your minds in Christ Jesus. (Philippians 4:7).

I have been made one with all who are in Christ Jesus.

There is neither Jew nor Gentile, neither slave nor free, nor is there male and female, for you are all one in Christ Jesus. (Galatians 3:28).

I have been blessed with every spiritual blessing in the heavenly places.

Praise be to the God and Father of our Lord Jesus Christ, who has blessed us in the heavenly realms with every spiritual blessing in Christ. (Ephesians 1:3).

I have been sealed with the Holy Spirit of promise.

And you also were included in Christ when you heard the message of truth, the gospel of your salvation. When you believed, you were marked in him with a seal, the promised Holy Spirit. (Ephesians 1:13).

God supplies all my needs.

And my God will meet all your needs according to the riches of his glory in Christ Jesus. (Philippians 4:19).

I am a citizen of heaven.

But our citizenship is in heaven. And we eagerly await a savior from there, the Lord Jesus Christ. (Philippians 3:20).

Invitation to the Thirsty

Come, all you who are thirsty, come to the waters; and you who have no money, come, buy and eat! Come, buy wine and milk without money and without cost. Why spend money on what is not bread, and your labor on what does not satisfy? Listen, listen to me, and eat what is good, and you will delight in the richest of fare. Give ear and come to me; listen, that you may live. I will make an everlasting covenant with you, my faithful love promised to David. See, I have made him a witness to the peoples, a ruler and commander of the peoples. Surely you will summon nations you know not, and nations you do not know will come running to you, because of the LORD your God, the Holy One of Israel, for he has endowed you with splendor. Seek the LORD while he may be found; call on him while he is near.

Let the wicked forsake their ways and the unrighteous their thoughts. Let them turn to the LORD, and he will have mercy on them, and to our God, for he will freely pardon. "For my thoughts are not your thoughts, neither are your ways my ways," declares the LORD. "As the heavens are higher than the earth, so are my ways higher than your ways and my thoughts than your thoughts. As the rain and the snow come down from heaven, and do not return to it without watering the earth and making it bud and flourish, so that it yields seed for the sower and bread for the eater, so is my word that goes out from my mouth: It will not return to me empty, but will accomplish what I desire and achieve the purpose for which I sent it. You will go out in joy and be led forth in peace; the mountains and hills will burst into song before you, and all the trees of the field will clap their hands. Instead of the thornbush will grow the juniper, and instead of briers the myrtle will grow. This will be for the

Orlease King

LORD's renown, for an everlasting sign, that will endure forever."

Isaiah 55:1-13

ABOUT THE AUTHOR

Orlease King is a Jamaican born entrepreneur with a Kingdom spirit. She is passionate about inspiring and motivating others and influencing positive change in the world.

Orlease owns two popular restaurants in Kingston, Jamaica (Reggae Mill Restaurant & OPA Greek Restaurant Limited). She is a customer service guru; a professional customer service trainer through the Customer Service Academy of Jamaica. She is highly service-oriented and passionate about offering people the best possible life experiences. Orlease aligns herself with movements that support making others feel accepted, empowered, and satisfied. She honors her position as a service provider through her belief in being a servant of God. "I am a servant of God. I work for Him, therefore, all my rewards come from Him."

AUTHORS NOTES

I have envisioned many things, most of which I accomplished. However, writing a book, let alone one that is geared towards leading persons to a better life, is not something I ever imagined I would do. But then there is a good explanation for not being able to see that as a reality. How was I to even consider leading anyone to a place of peace, hope, and eternal joy, if I was not on that journey myself? It is impossible to properly lead others if you do not know where you are going yourself.

Throughout my entire life I have always known there is a God and I always thought I loved Him. Yet I always made my own choices and decisions about what is best for my life, without consulting Him. I limited my prayers to: "Our Father, who art in heaven…" My knowledge of His Word went no further than the 23rd Psalm. I chose to act based on my emotions and what others say, instead of allowing God to guide me. I blatantly ignored the fact that I do not belong to myself (maybe you can relate). That type of life disqualifies us from the benefits of a great life.

Fortunately, it does not disqualify us from the love of God. He loves us regardless of our mess. It was that love that found me in a state of confusion and rescued me. Then I was able to hear God speak and follow His instructions and I eventually found the right path.

Today I can boldly say:

I KNOW WHO I AM!

I KNOW WHOSE I AM!

I KNOW WHERE I AM GOING!

AND I AM TAKING YOU WITH ME!

Orlease N. King

Notes

www.ingramcontent.com/pod-product-compliance
Lightning Source LLC
LaVergne TN
LVHW021408080426
835508LV00020B/2500